The Moment Coming

SELECTED ANAGRAMS: for *Grace*

choirmaster task rag
thermistor saga rack
taskmaster roach rig
magistrate rash cork
aristocrat shark gem
trickster orgasm ha a
trickster orgasm ah a
trickster aroma shag
trickster harm ago as
trickster ash arm go a
trichrome rat gas ask
strategic shark or ma
strategic harm ask or
strategem scar irk oh
strategem rock hairs
strategem hack sir or
shirtmake castor rag
shirtmake gator scar
shirtmake cargo rats
shirtmake star car go
rightmost scare ark a
rightmost sack rear a
rightmost sac era ark
registrar smack oath
registrar hack atoms
registrar sack hot ma
registrar mock hats a
registrar ham cot ask
ostracism great hark
orchestra stigma ark
orchestra mark gas it
orchestra grim ask at
orchestra kit gas arm
matriarch stroke sag
matriarch stork sage
matriarch gross take
matriarch task ogres
matriarch rot keg ass
masochist garter ark
margaret christakos
histogram crater ask
histogram aster rack
histogram trek scar a
greatcoat smirk rash
greatcoat marsh risk
greatcoat risks harm
catharsis remark got
catharsis mortar keg
artichoke smart rags
artichoke grass tram
trackage mortar hiss
trackage trash rim so
trackage smart sir ho
trackage short arm is
trackage shirt roams
trackage mirth ass or
trackage stir sham or

trackage rash mortis
trackage hiss rot ram
trackage hits arms or
thoriate marks crags
theorist karma crags
theorist mask rag ark
theorist rack mar gas
thematic grass ark or
theatric orgasm arks
theatric mark sags or
tamarack resort sigh
tamarack sight err so
tamarack shirt gores
tamarack horse grist
tamarack ghost sir er
tamarack toss rig her
tamarack rest sir hog
tamarack grits she or
tamarack she rots rig
straight coarse mark
straight smear croak
straight smack ear or
straight score karma
straight macro rakes
straight sore rack ma
straight sock rare ma
straight soar rack me
straight sera rock am
straight sear cork ma
straight scar amok re
straight race mask or
straight coma err ask
straight ask arc or me
stigmata shack error
stigmata rock rash re
shortage trick ram as
shortage smirk cart a
shortage skirt car ma
shortage sick rat ram
shortage scat mar irk
shortage risk cat arm
shortage cram ski art
shamrock striate rag
shamrock regatta sir
shamrock strait rage
shamrock target sari
shamrock satire trag
shamrock gratis rate
shamrock arrest gait
shamrock tiger star a
shamrock tater rig as
shamrock start rage i
shamrock great art is
shamrock grata tiers
shamrock rest tag air
shamrock star rage it
shamrock tit rag eras

shamrock gas art it er
schemata stark rig or
schemata risk rot rag
rhetoric karma tags
rhetoric mask tar sag
rhetoric stag mark as
rhetoric skat gas arm
rheostat cigar marks
rheostat sick ram rag
rheostat cram rig ask
restrict graham soak
restrict karma sag ho
restrict rash oak gam
restrict ask arm ha go
resistor hark gam act
resistor hack tag arm
mattress croak rig ah
mattress cargo irk ha
mattress hair cog ark
mattress char rig oak
matrices shark groat
matrices gator harks
matrices gosh tar ark
massacre girth ark to
massacre tart irk hog
marriage trash stock
marriage torch tasks
marriage shock tarts
isotherm track rag as
isotherm crag tar ask
homesick tartar rags
homesick star rat rag
gossamer trick art ah
gossamer tract hark i
gossamer itch tar rat
gossamer arch tit ark
gossamer char tar kit
crossarm right take a
crossarm eight ark at
crossarm rage hat kit
crossarm irk hat get a
chromate grass irk at
chromate irks gas art
chastise mark rot rag
charisma stork great
charisma gator treks
charisma star rot keg
charisma rest got ark
carriage stork maths
carriage stark moths
astigmat shack error
asterisk torch rag ma
asterisk march tar go
asterisk charm argot
asterisk harm got car
arrogate starch skim
arrogate tricks hams
arrogate skirt chasm
arrogate mirth sacks
arrogate match risks

arrogate march skits
armchair streak togs
armchair gasket rots
armchair trek got ass
armchair toss keg art
armchair gets arks to
archaism stroke trag
archaism task got err
archaism tart kegs or
trigram throes sack a
trigram stketch soar a
trigram socket rash a
trigram skater chaos
trigram sector ask ha
trigram scathe ark so
trigram rocket sash a
trigram racket ass ho
trigram assort heck a
trigram ashore stack
trigram track shoe as
trigram torch sea ask
trigram teach asks or
trigram store shack a
trigram stoke crash a
trigram stock era ash
trigram steaks roach
trigram stack horse a
trigram stack hero as
trigram short cake as
trigram shock aster a
trigram shock sea rat
trigram shark toe sac
trigram shake scar to
trigram shack tear so
trigram scare hot ask
trigram roast cask he
trigram retch oak ass
trigram heart sock as
trigram hater sack so
trigram ethos racks a
trigram earth cask so
trigram creaks oaths
trigram creak hot ass
trigram crash toe ask
trigram chokes star a
trigram chaos task re
trigram actor she ask
trigram toss hack ear
trigram toss ache ark
trigram task scar hoe
trigram tack rose ash
trigram sore chat ask
trigram sock rash tea
trigram sect hark so a
trigram scat hero ask
trigram scar sake hot
trigram echo asks art
trigram she ask actor
trigram her cat ask so
traitor charge masks

traitor smack shag re
traitor shack germs a
traitor grass heck ma
traitor mask crag she
tractor shriek gas am
tractor rakish games
tractor geisha marks
tractor garish ask me
tractor smash irk age
tractor shark images
tractor shame risk ga
tractor harem ski sag
tractor skim gash ear
tractor sigh mark sea
tractor rage kiss ham
tractor mask heir gas
tractor make gash sir
tractor kiss harm age
tractor sag irks me ha
tractor gem ass ark hi
trachea orgasm skirt
trachea smart risk go
trachea gross mark it
trachea star smog irk
trachea risk got arms
trachea grim rot asks
totemic rash rags ark
tigress mortar hack a
tigress macho art ark
tigress karma chat or
tigress charm rat oak
tigress actor hark ma
tigress oath mark car
tigress arch amok art
thicket grass roar ma
thicket roar mass rag
thicket rag ass arm or
teacart smirk rash go
teacart gross irk ham
teacart ram irks hogs
striate graham rocks
striate shock rag mar
striate harms cram go
stretch aroma irk gas
stretch saga mark or i
stretch roar magi ask
stretch mark sag or i a
stretch ask arm air go
storage starch irk ma
storage trick harm as
storage track his arm
storage mirth rack as
storage chasm irk art
storage charm risk at
storage sick harm rat
storage scar harm kit
storage rash mark tic
stomach gratis ark re
stomach garter risk a
stomach skat rear rig
stomack skit rare rag
stomach risk rage art
stearic graham stork
stearic trash mark go
stearic hark got arms
somatic grater shark
somatic stag hark err
smother tragic ark as
smother gratis rack a
smother track gas air
smother cigar tar ask
smother saga cart irk
smother risk rag cat a
smother rack gas art i
shatter smirk cargo a
shatter micro gas ark
shatter magic arks or
shatter macro sag irk
shatter croak grim as
shatter cargo risk ma
shatter risk coma rag
shatter marks cog air
shatter crag amok sir
shatter mar cog ark is
sarcoma target shirk
sarcoma streak right
sarcoma skater girth
sarcoma gather skirt
sarcoma stark grit eh
sarcasm threat irk go
sarcasm trite hog ark
sarcasm tiger hark to
sarcasm trio hair keg
sarcasm trek oath rig
sarcasm that ogre irk
sarcasm tit her ark go
sarcasm irk get art oh
roister track shag ma
roister chasm tag ark
roister sack harm tag
roister mart hack gas
roister mark chat gas
roister mack gash tar
roister hack tags arm
rickets orgasm rat ah
rickets orgasm rat ha
rickets orgasm art ha
rickets orgasm art ah
rickets mortar gash a
rickets graham roast
riskets asthma rag or
rickets aghast mar or
rickets trash arm ago
rickets smart rag oh a
rickets short rag a ma
rickets roast rag ham

DEFINITIVES

trickster orgasm ha a catharsis remark got

resistor hack tag arm homesick star rat rag

trigram actor she ask stretch saga mark or i

sarcasm that ogre irk rickets orgasm art ah

ALSO BY THE AUTHOR

Poetry

Not Egypt
Other Words for Grace

Chapbooks

missing/harsher sentences
With All My Heart I Heard You Speaking

THE MOMENT COMING

Poems by Margaret Christakos

ECW PRESS

The publication of *The Moment Coming* has been generously supported by
The Canada Council, the Ontario Arts Council, and the Government of
Canada through the Book Publishing Industry Development Program.

Canadian Cataloguing in Publication Data

Christakos, Margaret
The moment coming

Poems.
ISBN 1-55022-362-3
I. Title.

PS8555.H675M65 1998   C811'.54   C98-931404-9
PR9199.3.C47M65 1998

Edited for the press by Michael Holmes.

Cover design by Bryan Gee.

Imaging by ECW Type & Art, Oakville, Ontario.
Printed by Marc Veilleux Imprimeur, Boucherville, Québec.
Distributed in Canada by General Distribution Services,
325 Humber College Blvd., Etobicoke, Ontario M9W 7C3.

Published by ECW PRESS,
2120 Queen Street East, Suite 200,
Toronto, Ontario M4E 1E2.
www.ecw.ca/press

ACKNOWLEDGEMENTS

My gratitude to all who have been with me to the growing house: to Bryan Gee, cherished partner and co-parent; to our beloved children Zephyr, Clea, and Silas, and to those who are helping us to raise them; to my midwives Merryn Tate, Arlene Vandersloot and Melida Jiminez; to helpers and friends Nora Regan, Marion Meyer, Nancy Chater, John Volpe, Tracy Jenkins, Athina Goldberg, and Karen Kiddell; to Markham Street, Toronto, Ontario, and the College Street promenade; to the inspirational students of my OCAD Creative Writing classes over the last six years, particularly Michael Barker; to the beaches, wooded paths, rocks, and sun-dappled cottages of Beach Bays Resort, Parry Sound, Ontario, and to Claire, Ariel, and Zephyr playing on the beach at sunset; to the other families at my son's daycare 1994–97; to the creative people at MIX: the magazine of artist-run culture, particularly Amy Gottlieb; to my parents, siblings and extended families, and to Bryan's family; to Demetra Christakos, for her inexhaustible generosity; to Wellington Heights and Ramsey Lake, Sudbury, Ontario; to bpNichol, who continues to inspire me; thank you all for your sustenance. Special acknowledgement to Mark Fawcett and Victoria Freeman, the other two directions in Bryan's and my parenting compass: together we map a more complete landscape of the contemporary post-nuclear family.

This book was realized with the publishing and editorial support of the people at ECW Press and grant monies received through the Writers' Reserve and Works-in-Progress programs of the Ontario Arts Council between 1994 and 1996. Thanks in particular to editor Michael Holmes.

4BG+ZCS
+MJHDAH
XOXOXOX

CONTENTS

SUDBURY

1.—3. THE HEIGHTS

Down

She walks down the hill, the three humps of the hill, to the
public school at the very bottom, in the very cradle of the valley.
She climbs home at lunchtime, too tired to eat when she gets
there. Watches TV in the basement with burnt grilled cheese,
tearing back the black film, half-drinking the pale orange sauce.
She wears shoes that have a shallower heel than toe, for health
reasons, to keep slightly more upright as she walks down the
hill, and its slope threatens to pull her into a run. The shoes
don't change much. The Heights prevail, casting her down their
depths each morning and afternoon. She pulls her body up the
last stretch anxious to watch the end of *Another World*. She sleeps
like a princess on top of a mountain of mattresses, irked by the
yank of the bottom of the hill that will win her back. Her thighs
could pull a ditched Volkswagen up to solid ground. She slides
one palm down inside the soft denim, fingering the grommet.
She agrees.

Up

Her body is a girl's figure with large thighs from hill climbing.
A daily measure that will serve her well when she loses herself
picking blueberries against an orange sun slipping inside the
horizon's pocket, agreeing to calamity. Getting lost up there.
She will climb out, head south, hitch-hike, sleep at the Val Karen
Motel, skip across the Moon River bridge singing the theme
song, past Bala, past the Iroquois Cranberry Growers, past
MacTier, move by night through the grounds of the CNIB retreat,
snore in her sleeping bag on the French, net smelts, count stars,
hiccup as the police cruiser carries her back over 69, so
corrupted it rides like a trench, back to the Heights, home again.

Middle

Grade nine is a half-hour walk with three more hills before first period. The official streets are hyphenated by paths through extra land, land nobody argued for when they surveyed the lots, when they arranged for mortgages. Surplus footage. She has the route committed to memory, every step, the boulder she slaps with her backward sole, pushes off from, the patches of soil she likes best, the green shoots to watch for, maple stems, graffiti, green bottle bottom stuffed in the earth, tossed-off Mars Bar wrapper, clover grove, car door, spruce bower, alley. Big striped glass like a pickerel eye hooked on the INCO smoke drifting overhead. Then through the rusted iron gate to the next paved hump of official hill that never wavers from the point of the route, high school, a brown rectangle set into the lowest dip of the highway, past Lily Creek.

4.–9. COLD LINKS

Rink

The loudspeakers advertise fetishes she'd rather keep private.
But then she's skating around the new ice singing at the top of
her lungs. She has a body, she realizes, which can move faster
than she's proven so far. In this crowd, with people linked in
clichéd social units, her independence is vivacious. The skate
blades carve out a refrain of her past and illustrate the future, so
economical. She glides and spins, and works her thighs to their
boney ambitions. When the rink monitor clears the ice, then
invites everyone back to skate in the opposite direction, she feels
like her narrative powers are coming undone and begins
thanking God for pop radio.

Chocolate Glazed

The sticky icing and the doughy bread improve on each other's
excesses. The huge stack sticks right up through the centre of
each donut, we play ring toss, we centre ourselves on the
certainty the two will fit together. Matchmakers in our heart of
hearts. We want people to find their place in the bigger world,
sail through the air and land luckily. All of the places we end up
when linked look like a regular donut, vanilla-coated in winter,
and in the middle, in the great defined hole, lies Sudbury. Later
it is even harder to see the hole for the chocolate.

Underpass

It is anything but a tunnel of love. It links sun-neutered streets
of houses to downtown where she goes to buy 45s and watch
Cineplex double bills. The smell of the fresh roasting popcorn
pulls her through the dank innards where she is suddenly
profoundly aware of her own gurgling interior processes.
Her skin is a forgotten sleeve, like the underpass.

The Heights

It is where the link between sex and language is secured, where she finds out the word for "staying up late, to . . ." The way they walk up and down the hill in reference to each other, not companions, not friends. A herd of co-climbers of the hill for lunch and then for after-school television. Watching the smoke plume across the slag horizon, gauging the colour, being private and then embarrassing each other to no end. Just to reach the top. Humiliation rules they all know, and of chief importance remains how to ante up.

CNIB

The halfway clock like a religion she genuflects at in fast forward, marching late toward the school, awkward about her p's and q's, about which preposition belongs where. The clock is a charitable beacon for self-punitive speed-walking and rearranging her alibis to allow for believable stupidities. The clock she checks aware of her sightedness, her eyes like two high beams linked to a frozen doe, about to get walloped. After the clock, she races to the lobby of her high school, panting, guilty, ready to see the light.

Gold and Green

Maple leaves forever ensconced in season after season of change. Now and again there is slush-crested snow and the rink where she skates to discover her links to the others, the gold and green girls and boys with large school letters on their jacket backs. The rest of the alphabet ditched for songs of exile she knows others have written after leaving. You have to leave to see the stack in all of its glory, and imagine it wedged sideways through the Elgin Street chute, the underpass she likes to travel through and talk about, to work her nerve up to sun again.

10.–23. REPUTATION

Sentences

She was an odd and nervous girl in her own mind, but others watched her aristocratic stride and thought of new ways to arrange their sentences before the banal things slipped undisguised into her air space. Her gait alone made it obvious that she craved words at their zenith. The sidelong glances she shot at the standard row of tacky stores and slum lawyers' offices on Queen East always referred directly and unfavourably to the palatial spaces given over to specialty books and Arts-and-Crafts living room ensembles shown off in the wood-grained shop interiors along Front, just west of the south market. Still her own sixties vinyl coat sleeves had no elegance beyond the acrylic paint smears hardened near their elbows and the frayed lining that fringed the backs of her chapped hands, and farther along, at the end of each of the small muscular fingers, was an eccentrically filed moon of nail that showcased the miniature wedge of orange sambal she'd stashed away during her passionate lunch at the Sri Lankan restaurant she'd grown to love. It was easy to know she did not match in traditional style the reputation that accrued to her, or why others reported her to express ferocious clarity instead of rumpled waifness, but it was not at all easy to know exactly how or why.

Theory

She had no words for herself sometimes, when others approached and spoke in the cuneiform tongue of theory, or when she suddenly found herself wanting the non-smoking section, above all, in high-priced French restaurants. There was a trick to wearing nylons that she had never grasped. It comforted her to be considered unintimidating. So it made her laugh when invitations to the most important vernissages showed up in her mail. Later the panic about what to wear and who to talk with set in. Television had taught her a useful repertoire of cover-ups, but the commercial breaks never arrived when she needed them. Instead she stared too often and without respite into the purple gullet of that moment of awkward silence that she hated so.

Term

It was several years before she realized the term was one word, spelled in one gasp, and not the soft and lounging, and highly subjective, assessment uttered by a tired New Sudburian housewife after the kids had been put to bed. Oh, how I would love a good mellow drama, she believed she heard the woman's thought bubble sigh, while her tired ankles arched backward unnaturally and prodded at the rug under the plaid couch and she rubbed her neck seductively until her feet returned wearing the fur-trimmed slippers she had stashed six inches in, just out of view.

Life

Now her life was full-blown, pumped with oxygen and air freshener. She shopped along the Hard Edge of the Queen West Village, stopped at the Express Café to use the phone and then blew kisses at herself in the bathroom while waiting for her pesto and sun-dried tomato bruschetta to crispen. Life was marvellous.

Edge

If the town could simply hurry up and grow out of its old name and legally change all the signage, perhaps saying she was from Sudbury to the suave southerners would take on a quaint retro air. It would have the whipped-cream snowy edge of the North Village, with rustic train tracks, bowling lanes still renting very collectable fifties bowling shoes, souvenir chunks of nickel, and bottled Sulphuric Air, the on-the-run breakfast of real Canadian heroes of the industrial age. The whole place would be chemical-drenched but pristine, a perfect historical getaway for Toronto's pooped professionals. She waited, but her patience was wearing thin.

Style

It was El Mercado and Pit's House of Treasures that represented the exotic rest of the planet in her little town. Her mother taught her to exclaim ecstatically at the handi-crafty genius, nothing less, of the Third World's artisans. Her mother was an artist too, and she, ever the dutiful daughter, felt like a Woodstock revivalist sitting under an umbrella in Bell Park proudly peddling mom's weaving and pottery while mom, in her unrelenting enthusiasm for the Arts, splashed cold coffee on the mayor. Mom, bless her, impressed her as the living end of style. From these mornings, she learned to sell it up. C'mon, let's see a little energy. Smile at the people, patronize the arts and crafts movement, support the women who've learned to paint! Even seen through the omnipresent yellow haze, Art was *good*, and Being an Artist was nothing short of grand.

Glimpse

Everyone in town knew the CP underpass smelled of piss and darkness. It was the only patently dangerous place to walk alone, and you had to hold your palms over your temples when you came out through the Elgin Street chute, back into daylight, in case jobless and bored — which amounted to, logically enough, full-bladdered — men were urinating absentmindedly from the railing above. She developed a distaste for the standard glimpse of glimmering pink cock she got too often at this moment. It ruined her shopping mood and she inevitably ended up instead at Woolworths for a chocolate glazed. Sugar was the best amnesiac she knew.

Syntax

There were so many words she learned the very year she left that place. When she returned for a visit, it seemed no one spoke them in a daily context. "Context" was such a word. Instead, there'd be a missed beat in her syntax, an inverted stutter that left her feeling like a dunce, although she was told to stop being so queenly. The words returned only on the bus ride back to the City, and then, with a vengeance that overwhelmed her, she tried to stop adding *ay* to the end of every second sentence. *You can't take blood from a stone. That's just the way it is ay.* The obligatory empathy that was natural for such a depressed town, with so many unemployed still reeling from the INCO layoffs the year before, was beginning to peel away from her, like an old skin. The new ceremony, "going home," began to make her feel naked, ousted and dumb.

Rhythm

Around the back of the schoolyard her friend would ask for advice about an alcoholic mother and then, congenially, invite her to guzzle gin in the canyon. She looked down at the steady, reliable knit-and-purl rhythm of her cream-coloured vest and wondered about her nipples, how slow they were, how pent up, like her heart. What if she just let it all hang? But she couldn't.

Classics

Kensington Market was thronged with cool-looking individuals. There was never any shortage. She got so used to buying saffron and lemongrass that parsley, unless certifiably organic, became an unthinkable waste of space. It wasn't the herbs themselves, it was the sensation of owning these things, of wearing them all the way home knowing you'd bump into friends from the Institute who knew their Classics but hadn't yet embarked on the Odyssey of International Cuisine, that gave her day a prime edge.

This ability to cite galangal root — *You've never tried it? Oh you must, you must!* — had almost as much sway as knowing Horkheimer, etc. Cultural criticism had become all the rage. She left them standing in her ethnic wake eating toast. Milquetoast.

Wealth

When you walk along the water's edge, you hear the crowd cheering from the Ship Deck Stage just as the ferryboat with its necessary cargo of uncouth tourists dissonant with whiskey and beer chasers glides in front of a huge magnanimous moon and the night can't help but feel so well-to-do. The evening overflows with good, fun-loving people who *belong* here. Immediately to the northwest, the Skydome splays its brash sodium canopy, knowing it deserves to relax, it's earned "casual," the people *love* it, this world-classness. Real wealth doesn't give a fuck. It's there now, permanent, a fathomable and desired clot in the City's flow.

Sign

The kind of quiet she lived with was like being trapped in a mine shaft. It was four days since the fight "happened," no survivors could be contacted, so the shaft was scheduled to be boarded up. A sign, "Danger, Stay Away," was the only appropriate conversation left. She talked this way to herself until she got bored and dozed off with her chin sagging and her thin shoulders slumped over, like an unpopular old barber's.

Exception

She was mystified and a little afraid of the arena, the rock 'n roll guts of it, and the poorly lit sexy moat of loading ports all around its oval perimeter. Canada Day was the exception, but she knew the annual one-day festival of *multicultural expression* was an adventure for the whole town, leaving everyone vulnerable and open to gaffes, and also, full: of won ton soup, moussaka, apple strudel, petaheh, cabbage rolls. There was such a fine turnout the red carpet got blotched and sugared, but this was expected. Her mother was having one of her best times all year. It was something to sing about.

Club

Words had never failed her so evidently before, except when she fell completely silent for four minutes in the middle of her UNICEF competition speech at the Odd Fellows' Club. But this time she bumbled, flubbed, muttered, contradicted herself and spoke outright nonsense. The Performance Art teacher couldn't explain the babble away and asked her, had she researched, frankly, had she prepared? Finally, she caved, she just didn't get it. Why would a guy call himself Horizontal? General Idea was overly "conceptual." She wasn't used to thinking that way, ay. For the rest of term, she threw herself into alluding to things. Her favourite line, delivered with a wink, became, *What's a "meta" for, Gord?*

24. BASIN

Sand bottom like a parent underfoot. In the water her ears were plugged. The girlfriends and boyfriends had gotten serious now. Life had to give up its secrets.

To think this lake went from liquid to ice and back for centuries. What a solution. A body you could dive into with the purple hip-hugger bikini. A solo rink you could monopolize. And out of it came regal pike and pickerel. You cast a line easily or auger a hole first, then place your bets.

Important how the CN tracks rimmed the north shore so that to get to Ramsey you have to pass the crossing. Masterful white automated arm declaring your safe distance from the hurricane-rush of train cars. How many have been crushed, overrun, stupidly sacrificed. Other idiots. Not you, there, safe, obeying the arm. Hotly waiting to reach water.

If you can imagine a bronzed cradle of rock. Pressed bellies, backs of legs, the bleached fine hair floating atop calves. A seating place in August.

Can you hear me over the outboard. Under the surface. Through the flurries. Beside the train's hurtle.

Even if you can never hear me, you are always there. Something.

Plugged secrets. Liquid bets. Safe water. Vinyl steaming.

She comes from each of their bodies, you know it. Sugar maple, weeping willow, poplar, birch, blue evergreen. Distant horizon, silhouetted slag, watercolour sky. All of the clothes that are passed on come September as the body gets bigger, finally leaves on the bus. Hips puff, stylistic shifts. Bringing up this year who: over under through beside. Ramsey turning to ice, back to hazel liquid, while her thighs dappled with sweat wait for the arm to lift.

25.–35. THE CROSSING

25. SAND SECRETS
26. TO BETS
27. IMPORTANT WATER
28. IF AUGUST
29. CAN HURTLE
30. EVEN SOMETHING
31. PLUGGED STEAMING
32. SHE LIFT

33. PARENT UNDERFOOT
(   )
   sand can lift august if she hurtle secrets

34. HER EARS
(   )
   she even if to lift something august bets

35. LIFE
(   )
   steaming can water sand secrets important hurtle plugged

THE SEATING PLACE

(NOT AIDED BY COMPUTER)

1. LAST WORDS

i.

In the years that follow her,
she uses a mirror to see her backside.
She presses her fingertips into lipstick
and prints whorls across envelope flaps.
She predicts the future with lines in her palm.

Under cover of night she is sensual
all hair and skin and slippery insides.
There is nothing she hasn't thought of.

ii.

How she counts is forward
unless balancing her budget.
She hesitates at the threshold of big parties
shocked at the social conglomerate.
She employs humour at the awkward gaps
where words themselves fail, the body
answers: a wave, a shrug, a hole-in-one.
She can lift her ears in two-four time.

iii.

Inner world where there is no screen
no edge to stop her falling. Formless
has no meaning before the rule
of absolute form. She wags her feet
as if swimming in beet juice, this
is the figure of the heart flailing
but not panicked. Just splashing.
Attractive in the sense that something outside it
notices.

iv.

When the abdomen becomes a seating place
we know computers rate second.
Comfort decides more than is easily
admitted. When the loaf is flipped
out of its steaming pan onto the waiting rack
it hits the base that brands it: to cool off
we lay facedown, our bellies absorb wrinkles,
we and she are striped like mammals, good camouflage.
The stomach investigates safety, to do this
effectively it must be bare, it must flatten,
must press against another.

v.

Across the lake she can make out
basic elements: rocks, trees, hills, fatigue,
her wincing eyeline. She says to her companion
I'll get some tea going, I've got muffins,
cheese, smoked fish. Come into my house
my bed, my body. Here is where I was first
touched, persuaded to sleep, here is my graduation
photograph. See my mother, my father. They sure
were a lot younger then.

vi.

her, backside. lipstick flaps. palm.

sensual insides. of.

forward budget. parties conglomerate.
gaps body hole-in-one. time.

screen Formless rule feet
this flailing splashing. it notices.

place second. easily flipped
rack off wrinkles, camouflage.
this flatten, another.

out fatigue, companion muffins,
house first graduation sure then.

FIRST WORDS

In she She and She
Under all There

How unless She shocked She where answers: She

Inner no has of as is but Attractive notices.

When we Comfort admitted. out it we we The effectively must

Across basic her I'll cheese, my touched, photograph. were

her, sensual forward gaps
screen this
place rack this
out house

HER SENSUAL FORWARD GAPS

Heard central forehead gasp/
Red looseness draw off spark:
approximate equivalents

Sorry, what did you say
sorry, what did you say

Say it again please
this time enunciate

Hearse and chew yule four word scab
surround, sound it out

Sorry what
sorry what
what juice, ay

Beet, like in the heart
the valves shut then
open

HEART THEN OPEN

No screen to stop her wide arc through water
it is the depths not shoreline
teaching limits here
   nothing square or pixillated
as the breath is sucked in, expelled

and she thinks of pushing the boy through
staying with him those many many months
the latter two days of labour
then minutes of surreal hope
(   )
as his fontanel adjusted to air
and his lips still kissed the channel
not understanding the function "to breathe" yet

those seconds when he was half-born
her mouth hanging wide, almost
screaming
everyone else smiling like maniacs
she felt it, her heart
then, open

EVERY FIFTH WORD

No wide is teaching or is

and the him the labour hope to still understanding yet

those half-born almost like her

HEART THEN OPEN: RETAINER

thos(e)
half-bor(n)
almos(t)
lik(e)
he(r)

2. PARTITIONED DAY

a.m. (dawn)

She sleeps moulded to her child
one elbow tenting his midriff, braided
lower bodies laid to rest beneath cotton, suggesting how
familial landscapes are delicate, and deserving of
protection.

Earlier she stumbled across quaint kitchen
linoleum cool, darkness syrupy
through which his cries jutted
birch branches quivering in fog
just the tips visible, and even moreso,
wholly divisible from the forest floor.

She thinks of a lone pine cone
any item that lives at the end
of a larger body and is likely, in fact, intended
to drop off.

a.m. (breakfast)

Nutrition is a subject for family psychologists

why be required to eat anything

why crave cleanliness

To her, the plateful of hot smells
says all there is to say about good
mothering.

p.m. (noon)

At twelve exactly the radio self-ignites,
ebola and Brian Wilson and Mexico: The Drug War
enter like mosquitoes until she swats the off
button. But quiet is a technology of the past. Her
inner world where there is no plug, no drainage
system, just overflow. Waves piling on the shore
like a rug being pulled out from under
by a manic magician, presto, presto, presto
ad infinitum. Screens of the cottage windows
matching the vibration of crickets. Chipmunks.

p.m. (coffee break)

In the city she and her co-workers would
break for coffee about three, about the time
the children are released. Maybe a sense memory
of after-school Kool-Aid, and allowing the babysitter
to be there.

After coffee the screen would slip again into that space
where another head might, in another era,
have appeared. The mouth might have moved
of its own accord. Her day might have been
more than a reflection of herself.

p.m. (dinner)

She skips dinner because the child
goes to sleep, so she
goes to sleep.

p.m. (dusk)

She extracts packages from the fridge:
cheese, smoked fish. Releases the seal
on the muffin tin, it pops, her palm lightly
moulds around the cool gummy head
of the muffin. That cake smell puffs up
and she salivates. The kettle begins to wail,
she half-spills the water, brings the tea in a thermos
to the sunroom.

The difference between dusk and dawn
is the condition of the body. In evening,
too vulnerable for words, coated with dust
and negative ions from the computer screen,
layered like a linen closet with fresh story items, really just
the day's worst coincidences, her body
teeters a little. She finds it difficult to stand,
so sleeps again, wearing the food inside, carrying it
sideways.

a.m. (midnight)

The two adult bodies have everything
and nothing to touch about. For the abdomens
to flatten and press together requires great
entanglement of the appendages, to say
little of the twin nervous systems, the genitals,
the hearts. Yes, to have the two concave half-moons
of the navels match up and matter the way
a full moon deeply matters to anyone looking
is as uncertain as citizens on opposite sides
of the planet synchronizing their watches.

Every twenty-four hours,
the inner clock strikes midnight
a few times, not once, don't you think

MID-POINTS

bodies laid to
birch branches quivering
the end of

a subject for
required to eat
why crave cleanliness
smells says all

is no plug,

time the children
appeared. The mouth

child goes to

head of the
a linen closet

hearts. Yes, to
strikes midnight a

TURNING BACK THE CLOCK

a midnight strikes
to Yes, hearts.

closet linen a
the of head

to goes child

mouth The appeared.
children the time

plug, no is

all says smells
cleanliness crave why
eat to required
for subject a

of end the
quivering branches birch
to laid bodies

THREE MIDNIGHTS

child

why

bodies

(were *a lot younger then*)

MINOR DREAMS

i. dream remembered near nightfall

dawn evening, dust screen,
just body stand, it sideways.

ii. a.m. radio déjà vu

self-ignites, Mexico: mosquitoes button.
of where drainage on
being a ad windows
Chipmunks.

iii. dream of first words, every third line

She familial linoleum just
any Nutrition To At button. like
matching the After of goes cheese,
of to too the sideways. to the is the

iv. dream of first letter every line, in seven-letter groupings (scrabble hands)

SOLFPEL	lopes
TBJWSAO	boat
TNWWTSM	ms
AEEBISL	eels
BAMIBTO	tomb
TAWHOMS	whoas
GGSCOMO	cogs
ASTTITA	stat
LTTSSTA	lasts
TELTOAI	total
OETA (3 wild) BSR	breast

v. dream planned for following night

breast (wild) total
lasts stat cogs
whoas tomb eels
ms boat lopes

3. THE OFFENDING EAR

/science

When water lodges in the inner ear
it is as if a screen dances
mad with static. And when you shake the head
you feel the brain's weight, substantial,
yet not big enough to move
the thimbleful of liquid out.
Only gravity can rectify such a blockage.
Not will, nor hope, nor breath
sucked from the outside by someone
else's lips. Just the decisiveness
of time, proportion, velocity. She can't
bear hearing this, though, and shuts out
the voice telling it.

The brain prides itself
on such solutions.

/marriage

The hope in the middle of the previous poem
keeps her hearing intact.

hear/ear/ring. She likes this.

The ear in the middle of the function
suffers blockage more than
is to be expected.

Her ring on the middle finger
chokes off feeling at appropriate moments
when she is already flushed

swollen, larger than life,
she doesn't hear the telephone ring,
the kettle whistle, she pretty much
hums.

When you hum the middle of the brain
feels on fire, or purple like an icicle
or pretty. It pretty much
describes itself. hum/um/ming.
She hears him through water,
his voice ricocheting in the shower stall,
sliding around the inside
of the white curtain. His shape seems as distant
as a thimbleful of water, aesthetically
pleasing, impossible to
dislodge.

/parapsychology

One ear blocked and one open
is a recipe for vision problems, as
the ear that can't hear asks the closest eye
to guide it. On the other side
all functions are normal so it is
in the middle, problems arise.
The nose gets confused too,
especially if one sinus is jammed up
and the other breathes free, and if this
is opposite to the blockage of the ear,
watch out.

HOPE: BY-PRODUCTS

i.

When water lodges in the inner ear
keeps her hearing intact.
the ear that can't hear asks the closest eye

you feel the brain's weight, substantial,
suffers blockage more than
in the middle, problems arise.

Only gravity can rectify such a blockage.
chokes off feeling at appropriate moments
and the other breathes free, and if this

else's lips. Just the decisiveness
she doesn't hear the telephone ring,
/

the voice telling it.
When you hum the middle of the brain
/

/
describes itself. hum/um/ming.
/

/
sliding around the inside
/

/
pleasing, impossible to
/

ii.

When ear keeps intact the eye

you substantial, suffers than in arise.

Only blockage. chokes moments and this

else's decisiveness she ring,

the it. When brain

describes hum/um/ming.

sliding inside

pleasing to

iii.

When Only the sliding
eye this brain inside

iv.

/   the sliding
/   brain inside

v.

Only blockage chokes moments

and this moves her forward
through the middle to a

and this defies her repeatedly
so she cuffs the offending ear
as

and this gives her the idea
she might offer a truce
but

~~and this is bitter~~

4. ACCIDENTS OF MODERN PRIVACY

She replays the video to check her backside,
assess how much space it takes
across the small screen. She presses
the viewfinder with its rubber cup
up to one eye, watches like a scientist
for irrefutable measure — there she is, over
half an inch wide! And there! The *ass* of her!

Minutes pass like this, her iris a mere
three inches from the tiny screen, rapt,
then is driven outside by nausea and heat,
the whole body stumbling down four stone steps
toward the sound of the lake muscling to shore,
an under-sized athlete obsessed with sit-ups, expert
tuck of the head to ankles, the breath
exhaled with such force and so often it percolates
foam, grey tableau with white about the edges,
a gush, a gushing noisescape in the dark.

She recognizes, then, that her ears bear up
a weakness of vision, that in one eye
what she sees is a flannel rectangular screen
like the stuffing inside a past favourite toy
suddenly obliterating the toy itself. When the love
object is smudged who can love it
the same? She slaps a palm over the good eye
to panic more fully, there it is, the print
of her interest in seeing her own ass!
Why had she cared so furiously, even saved
the moment after the child fell to sleep
for this? Why did she crave the camera's proof?

She can see again the next morning,
well enough to track the thrumming sound
above her to the small body that makes it,
a hummingbird hanging over her head
as if stalled there, administering itself
to the middle of her cured eye. Its wings thrash about
in the frame of the disappeared screen
shadowing the whole city that lurks there, the tools
she can use to know herself better,
much more exactly, than her ancestors ever dreamt.

BLOCKED VIEWS

She replays the video to check her backside,

assess	takes
across	presses
the	cup
up	scientist
for	over

half an inch wide! And there! The *ass* of her!

Minutes pass like this, her iris a mere

three	rapt,
then	heat,
the	steps
toward	shore,
an	expert
tuck	breath
exhaled	percolates
foam,	edges,

a gush, a gushing noisescape in the dark.

She recognizes, then, that her ears bear up

a	eye
what	screen
like	toy
suddenly	love
object	it
the	eye
to	print
of	ass!
Why	saved
the	sleep

for this? Why did she crave the camera's proof?

She can see again the next morning,

well	sound
above	it,
a	head
as	itself
to	about
in	screen
shadowing	tools
she	better,

much more exactly, than her ancestors ever dreamt.

COMPOSITE VIEW (AFTERTHOUGHT)

Much more exactly, than her ancestors ever dreamt.
She can see again the next morning,
for this? Why did she crave the camera's proof?
She recognizes, then, that her ears bear up
a gush, a gushing noisescape in the dark.
Minutes pass like this, her iris a mere
half an inch wide! And there! The *ass* of her!
She replays the video to check her backside.

5. ASSUMING THE READY

i.

Closing shutters to protect the inner world
from the outer too-wild one, she notes the screens
though camouflaged sit just inside wooden slats,
part and parcel of the cottage.
Her cottaged life, viewed and breathed
through the sieves of safety
she installs everywhere. Gridded crosshairs
orienting how she comes in contact with anyone
on the outside. Maybe it is just enough
to feel heat emanate.

A voice moves through wire handily, also.

Speak to me in darkness, so the fine
grains of tenor solace reach me.

When your abdomen touches, I become fully
confessional.

ii.

There was a time when the child
fluttered inside, large moth heavy with the weight of rain
travelling toward light at the screen's
backside. Here, the prospect
of warmth was titillating to the point
of frenzy, which provides its own hot aura.

There are reports of women who just thought
they had a bad case of chronic heartburn.
When the baby burst through
relief looked surprisingly like panic.

iii.

She can't quite believe she let her guard drop
completely ushered the semen upward, unscreened
freak storm of nature like the waterfall
that flows in reverse.

Suspending disbelief is the true magic.

(READY) OR (NOT)

i.

Closing to the world
from outer one, notes screens
though sit inside slats,
part parcel the
Her life, and
through sieves safety
she everywhere. crosshairs
orienting she in with
on outside. it just
to heat

A moves wire also.

Speak me darkness, the
grains tenor reach

When abdomen I fully
confessional.

ii.

There a when child
fluttered large heavy the of
travelling light the
backside. the
of was to point
of which its hot

There reports women just
they a case chronic
When baby through
relief surprisingly panic.

iii.

She quite she her drop
completely the upward,
freak of like waterfall
that in

Suspending is true

(NOT) OR (READY)

i.

shutters protect inner
the too-wild she the
camouflaged just wooden
and of cottage.
cottaged viewed breathed
the of
installs Gridded
how comes contact anyone
the Maybe is enough
feel emanate.

voice through handily,

to in so fine
of solace me.

your touches, become

ii.

was time the
inside, moth with weight rain
toward at screen's
Here, prospect
warmth titillating the
frenzy, provides own aura.

are of who thought
had bad of heartburn.
the burst
looked like

iii.

can't believe let guard
ushered semen unscreened
storm nature the
flows reverse.

disbelief the magic.

TWO FLOWS IN REVERSE

i.
magic. reverse. the unscreened guard like burst heartburn.
thought aura. the prospect screen's rain the become me.
fine handily, emanate. enough anyone Gridded of breathed
cottage. wooden the inner

ii.
true in waterfall upward, drop panic. through chronic just
hot point the the of child confessional. fully reach the also.
heat just with crosshairs safety and the slats, screens world

FILTERED WATERS

(every sixth word)

i.
magic. burst screen's handily, breathed

ii.
true through the the safety

(every fifth word)

i.
magic. like the become enough cottage.

ii.
true panic. point confessional. heat and

(every fourth word)

i.
magic. guard thought screen's me. enough breathed inner

ii.
true drop just the fully heat safety screens

DISTILLATE

breathed safety
cottage. and
inner screens

6. PATENT

i.

H   C
OFF   ON   OFF

When the perfect mix to warm
streams parallel to the spine
she comes alive. Memory is like this
echo of the similar, word and deed.

To tuck the knees under the breath
and hold it, this is what the bitch nurse
wants of her, four in the morning
and through a screen of pain so voluminous
it sifts through her like pride, dark sweep
of her cells, an army passing.

The contract she defends is with herself, its
minute details she studies
as if checking a life raft for holes
before throwing it all overboard, everything
she needs for a new future sails over the edge
and then she leaps, feetfirst
followed by the chin, the whole body knuckle perfect
as the stainless steel point slices between vertebrae
and cord and the sea shall hold you
if you only let it.

ii.

What she does, finally, is not
aided by computer or hardware

no compass aimed at the horizon

nothing foolproof
except pain and
love (headfirst slide
toward scissors,
oxygen

iii.

The rhythm of water
bashing at all sides of an island
is accostive, it takes over the centre

what can soothe at the start
accelerates to a huge backside ache, a new
cold wound the size of a ripe plum,
ripped a bit

midwives help, they say
no one tells you
it'll feel like a hot poker up the ass
its good to know this
in advance

iv.

She revels occasionally in the perfect mix
of hot and cold, fully adjustable,
streaming down from the showerhead
on hair and skin and slippery outsides
alive with thinking. So lyrical, banal as
a cured asshole, warm middle of her abdomen
unbroken, too. Buoyed up always
by the child, almost three years from the root
now high as her hipline the fontanel
covered over and hat-brimmed.

v.

Swept?
Lights out?

vi.

her abdomen unbroken, too
the size of a ripe plum, headfirst
slide toward scissors,
this echo of the similar,

vii.

He — the man — fingers her wrists like dials
working to adjust anything
in his power trying to aid
in the end just counting
and gazing

thirty-three hours

the son's body, mid-slide between escape
and arrival streams parallel to her spine, purple cord
suddenly evident like a memory
of the both of them, mixed up in sex
scissored clean, a new patent to register
and puzzling, this he she and he
hard to handle at first — another
abdomen in the middle, the triplet
hearts

GAZING

i.

When warm streams spine she this echo deed.
To breath and nurse wants morning and voluminous it sweep of
    passing.
The its minute studies as holes before everything she edge and
    feetfirst followed perfect as vertebrae and you if it.

ii.

What not aided hardware
no horizon
nothing foolproof except and love slide toward scissors, oxygen

iii.

The water bashing island is centre
what start accelerates new cold plum, ripped bit
midwives say no you it'll ass it's this in advance

iv.

She mix of adjustable, streaming showerhead on outsides alive
    as a abdomen unbroken, always by root now fontanel
    covered hat-brimmed.

v.

Swept? Lights out?

vi.

her too the headfirst slide scissors, this similar,

vii.

He dials working anything in aid in counting and gazing
thirty-three hours
the escape and cord suddenly memory of sex scissored register
   and he hard another abdomen triplet hearts

COUNTING (i. – vii.)

When deed. to passing. the it.
What hardware no horizon nothing oxygen
The centre what bit midwives advance
She hat-brimmed.
Swept out?
her similar,
He gazing thirty-three hours the hearts

7. A VOICE MOVES HANDILY, ALSO

When she holds her own forehead
it has the heat of rock to offer
curved composite of her parents' foreheads
and the hand, which thinks of them always

trolling over rock, sand, water, held up
to campfire smoke and coals, piercing
the plump wiener down its wiggly length, hard
for the men to do this she thinks in private
feeling heroic roasting hot dogs on green twigs
for children, it takes so little

as long as they are noticed, talked to, touched
with care while warm washcloth strokes
explain judiciously to fingers, cheeks, chins why
cleanliness is required, how germs don't take
holidays, how the body will feel
better, believe us

belief in each other is the first danger
of families, that trust that crosses overhead
like the shadow of a bushplane, drone
of worry, heavy flying thing at high noon
that could drop out of the sky
if handled badly

how the sky for the most part floats
parallel to the water, two navy abdomens
matching half-moons on enough nights every month
to stay intimate on the pitch-dark ones
when it is impossible for palms to
find the forehead of either one

FOREHEAD

When she holds her own forehead
trolling over rock, sand, water, held up
as long as they are noticed, talked to, touched
belief in each other is the first danger
how the sky for the most part floats

PALM

and the hand, which thinks of them always
for children, it takes so little
better, believe us
if handled badly
find the forehead of either one

LIKE ABDOMENS TOUCHING

When she holds her own forehead
find the forehead of either one

trolling over rock, sand, water, held up
if handled badly

as long as they are noticed, talked to, touched
better, believe us

belief in each other is the first danger
for children, it takes so little

how the sky for the most part floats
and the hand, which thinks of them always

8. KEYBOARD

(e)

every morning she spends on the rock, series
of screens inside her gradually fading
what the sun feels like unblocked
almost unbearable

(n)

not so nearly a refuge or escape
swirling water tantalizes, as if the body's
insides implore to swim around
unsuited

(t)

to the north her birthplace, to the south
a metropolis, under her ass is moss
and last night, meteors, flashlights,
children worrying about bears

(r)

retaining anonymity in the bush she sees
the son and husband in a canoe pushing paddles
through blueberry-coloured waves, stroking sky and water
and waving toward the beloved lump of rock,
sure they see her

STENOGRAPH i: first pass

(every second word)

every she on rock, of inside gradually what sun like almost
not nearly refuge escape water as the insides to around
to north birthplace, the a under ass moss last meteors, children
    about
retaining in bush sees son husband a pushing through waves,
    sky water waving the lump rock, they her

(every third word)

every spends rock, screens gradually the like unbearable
not a escape tantalizes, the implore around
to her the metropolis, ass and meteors, worrying
retaining the sees and a paddles waves and waving beloved rock,
    see

(every fourth word)

every on of gradually sun almost
not refuge water the to
to birthplace, a ass last children
retaining bush son a through sky waving lump they

(every fifth word)

every the inside the almost
not or as implore
to to under and children
retaining she husband paddles sky toward rock,

STENOGRAPH i: second pass

every she on rock of inside gradually what sun like almost
not a escape tantalizes, the implore around
to birthplace, a ass last children
retaining she husband paddles sky toward rock,

every spends rock, screens gradually the like unbearable
not refuge water the to
to to under and children
retaining in bush sees son husband a pushing through waves,
    sky water waving the lump rock, they her

every on of gradually sun almost
not or as implore
to north birthplace, the a under ass moss last meteors, children
    about
retaining the sees and a paddles waves and waving beloved rock,
    see

every the inside the almost
not nearly refuge escape water as the insides to around
to her the metropolis, ass and meteors, worrying
retaining bush son a through sky waving lump they

STENOGRAPH i: third pass

every rock gradually like a the to ass
    retaining paddles rock
not the to children bush husband through
    water lump her rock the
to the ass meteors, retaining and waves
    beloved every gradually
retaining a waving every the nearly water
    insides to metropolis, meteors

STENOGRAPH i: fourth pass

rock like the ass paddles
not to bush through lump rock
to ass retaining waves every
retaining waving the water to meteors

STENOGRAPH ii: first pass

(every sixth word)

every rock, gradually like
not escape the around
to the ass meteors
retaining sees a waves, waving rock

STENOGRAPH ii: second pass

rock, like escape
around the meteors
sees waves, rock

9. WHAT SHE KNOWS

ass and meteors, worrying
how best to enter the tent city
of her stomach, tightly pegged
words unsaid because zipped in
under tongue, what metropolis
can survive unaided by
computer now, she craves her screen
more than a hot shower

out here cottage life
breathes windily, elemental
rock, water, trees, fatigue
her wincing body arranged in a chair
the companion gone sailing
on a borrowed sloop, sweet child
sleeping off lunchtime's great unsolved
mysteries, how to unlock the door
spoon yoghurt unmessily
change out of a sweatshirt,
all the projects that
make or wreck the spirit
by mid-afternoon

when she graduated her parents
surprised her and came,
travelled south on a milk-run
bus route, forfeited lunch to
get there on time, claimed seats,
sat in steam, clapped handily
made sure she had the photograph
to show you, so you would touch her
gradually supplant the screen
she'd carried since girlhood
on her midriff

how to touch abdomens
on the moonless nights, when the heart
is flipped on its back and
flailing like a bug, too stupid
to roll over and live again,
this is the question that can wreck
or make her by dinnertime
she knows it
knows plenty

FIRST WORDS

ass how of words under can computer more

out breathes rock, her the on sleeping mysteries, spoon change
all make by

when surprised travelled bus get sat made to gradually she'd on

how on is flailing to this or she knows

LAST WORDS

plenty it dinnertime wreck again, stupid and heart abdomens

midriff girlhood screen her photograph handily seats, to
    milk-run came, parents

mid-afternoon spirit that sweatshirt, unmessily door unsolved
    child sailing chair fatigue elemental life

shower screen by metropolis in pegged city worrying

EVERY FIFTH WORD

ass can rock, mysteries, by get she'd flailing knows
plenty stupid girlhood seats, mid-afternoon door fatigue
by worrying

KNOWS FLAILING SHE'D GET BY, MYSTERIES

she prints on envelope flaps whorls of fingertips
examines her palm, watches her backside
under night's cover she touches whatever.

counting up days to come she starts from yesterday
enters rooms slowly trying to laugh
when words fail, reads people's ear lobes.

just splashing, she notices comfort.

WHORLS

i.

whatever. touches she cover night's under
backside her watches palm, her examines
fingertips of whorls flaps envelope on prints she

lobes. ear people's reads fail, words when
laugh to trying slowly rooms enters
yesterday from starts she come to days up counting

comfort. notices she splashing, just

ii.

night's under whatever. touches she cover
her examines backside her watches palm,
prints she fingertips of whorls flaps envelope

words when lobes. ear people's reads fail,
rooms enters laugh to trying slowly
up counting yesterday from starts she come to days

splashing, just comfort. notices she

iii.

envelope prints palm, her cover night's
days up slowly rooms fail, words

she splashing,

iv.

splashing, she

words fail, rooms slowly up days
night's cover her palm, prints envelope

v.

splashing, she
words days
night's envelope

10. THE ENVELOPE
(or, *Words Fail Night's Cover*)

Grey screen that sifts the view
printed now on the backside of the brain
unreadable, and remembering
no good reason to limit technology's
hold on the imagination she refers
to other mirrors she has trusted

the silence of negative ions sparkling on dust
absorbed like a new food group
into the upper chest, unfamiliar lump
swallowed alongside the pink taste of rock, private
shoreline, train roaring behind the cottage,
pine needles, lichen, blue heron stories

and waves from the wooden raft, rectangular grid
afloat in the bay's middle
sturdy porous platform they all swim toward
climb onto, willingly
wear as an anchor
for their own nature

      she he and he
      he she and he
      he he and she

all hair and skin and slippery again
as if floating in that juicy inner city

not quite ready to cast the body out,
feel the warm wet seating place of her abdomen
rise up on the outside, the parents' hands fluttery
and cool against your forehead, like a fine screen
through which you are bound
from that moment forward
to see the world

THE SEAL
(or, The Body Answers)

Grey brain unreadable, technology's hold trusted

the group into private shoreline, stories

and middle sturdy willingly wear nature

she he he again as

out, feel fluttery and bound from world

BRINGING YOU UP

for Zephyr

BRINGING YOU UP

I take you by the hand and pull you
yank like I am ferocious
& really meaning it I squeeze
the cloth at the back of your shoulderblades into handles
to lift you

so you will move

you will
move if
I have to carry you the whole goddamned way so help me

I have a well planned day of definitives:
to get to the bank machine streetcar you to daycare
then to work this
I plan things
to work smoothly

& your legs know how to move things up in the world
a small chopper raising fury I catch on my shoulder
bawling head first no no nor justice

just one heart muscling in the gutter
how far mine sinks before boarding us both
to meet triumph in the driver's eye
where I see ourselves merely
a bright mess of primary wills
before that steely & incontrovertible
look you give the public
bringing your mother up for scrutiny yes
up to something measurably
good again

MUSCLING

What the arms can do for you
now that you are thirty-four pounds
one third my ideal weight
one quarter the real thing I have become
quite impossible

What I can lift to my chin to kiss half asleep

What I can wrestle from sidewalks
when you pretend to be mineral

What I hold clear of you when the shit hits my hand
& I loathe it
the shit I hold in like a muscle structure
well-toned at the Y I am this wholly
abdominal character
evolving

With every repetition this body impresses me to
no end
how I carry you one kilometre in the snow without coffee
or chocolate
without sex in the morning or the squeaky clean night
before
when what matters is the obviousness of exhaustion
exhausted
how the brain's role in reproduction really must be
debated
until inevitably on this matter the eyelids
flit up
down

the set ending

THE SHIT

After fourteen hours
the midwife suggests an enema
to make more room for you

as if all the shit in my life up to now
is on its way out

& in its place you will come

WAY OUT

For example I could live on another planet
but nursing would suffer
& the milking blister on your top lip
would deflate

harder to begin again with a fresh perspective

Close up to you
I can't find a way out of your gaze
brown universe where all colour visiting
decides to stay becoming
some of your spectral
vision

That for now sums me up my usual
in-your-face attitude on your way back from sleep
be assured I'm there again
milking you awake
& gazing

no way out of me
though you may wish it someday

SUFFER

The pink blaze of your buttocks punishes
me too, though you feel it realer
cries reeling from your mouth
sobs that turn to coughing

The special blanket, well operated, wraps you up
its hand-sewn stitches hold you together
though our friend made it, not me
disarmed for months now
by suffusion in the red nakedness
you present to me three hours later
again I'm so sorry

I couldn't sew a thing
except this burn of lousy mothering
to my cheek
the red one on each side you
see me wearing nothing at all through

yet hold me to the moment coming
when pain stops &
suffers our excesses such
little children together
rashbummed
rougefaced
wrapped in blankets

Hair of the womb that
bit us one and the same, what's
the difference

THE MOMENT COMING

What precipitousness there is between the words moment &
mom
the eternity I've slipped into

sperm into the egg

on mutual orgasm my baby
finger into his ear
which made the occasion particularly memorable
him plugged up, ready to pop
me laying in the member

neither of us having been exactly so obvious before
about the universal
symmetries
you will unhinge

PLUGGED

Or the other words
pacified
soothed
by silicone
those two bits of my body
infinitely reproducible
insertable
suckleable
if you just say the word
the loud one
the waah
a whole industry will answer

BITS

Holding ourselves back is de rigueur
your mouth on my breast could bite as easily
& I could swell with erotic desire

or vanish, instead

You coax me toward the common interest
the human problem of growing up
gradually
drag me by one nipple to a reckoning
with how sexy we are

soft breast your eye is up against constantly
eunuch skin of your cheek, bellows I adore
in a cycle of puffing, sucking
chuffing like a pony's nostril as it labours
around the demands of a premature bridle
this new & more appropriate morality
where my tit is a temple now
around which we gather & gaze & supplicate

The suspense of feeling
is killing me sometimes I think
I will forget where I'm leading you, lapse

& feel it

& have to pull you off quickly
away from who I've been in the world up till now
before I installed my heart in my mouth
& came here like a virgin
to serve you

SUSPENSE

Your body giggles in the jumping device
in practical bliss as we've planned it
cushion catching your ankles
springing you back up to weightlessness
& so it goes

the kind of parenting we provide as we scuttle
in the sheets, ass-naked & deliberate
about) arousal (we have forgotten everything
outside the parentheses of platonic love
or do it badly now

only one eye each on the other's hard on
the second consumed in your all-seeing gaze

whose dear focus the sight of us like this might
split irremedially
despite the consensual barricade of pillows
we try to protect each other's fucking
huge genitals from bouncing up over
while still enthusiastically pursuing what
we did to make you

not knowing whether you will ever let us

find it again

HUGE

As you come through the canal
I feel like a football player, huge neck muscles
hauling my entire brain far down
to where it lived in primordial days
in the pelvis
near the sacrum
shaped like an infant's head
ringed with caput, cartilaginous against
the forces of history coming

The history that will make it ascend, board its
evolutionary lift up through the torso and ribcage
squeeze past the heart, underfed apatosaurus with its metre
running out, nudging it off kilter, then
dull & overstuffed for a few centuries
idle at the throat, a calcifying lump not quite sure
of its trajectory,

if there even is one

if it's worthy

how the hell it got here

until reverse hydraulics begin squashing
beyond grunts more like modern linguistics it
bursts through to the roominess
inside the back of the head
my entire head readied like a hand
about to cast you out the top

giant whistle into oxygen

for the first time

THE HELL

Of seeing your father in you
when I am angry at him
your eyes flashing from side to side
between us

SEEING

Things in the public park we attend
are deteriorating

The government cares little about
those who are wageless

Pigeons and squirrels appear to be
living with AIDS

Your fingers wrap right around the elephant
handlebars

& your feet hold you vertical

I see you
at the top of the slide
the high one
gleaming

I Fucked Maria boasts the wall

Fuck'n Shit For Brains sings the jungle gym

I see you

BRAINS

Rather than brawn
to make a man of you
I choose the story of how I skated
around a lake at night
searching for love

In high school I had so many
brains in my head
I couldn't speak
& gave these smiles to boys
meaning I can never have you
can I

small yawn in my lap
your intelligent brain over
my intelligent cunt
I want to graft you to me
as if you won't become
soon enough

one of the inpenetrable

NIGHT

Songs I make up for you are sung then
a dark voice is how you will remember me
if I should die before you wake

If something should happen to you
these are the songs I will remember you laying by
a night without light never able to sing
in the dark again

If you should travel beyond my voice
I shall find you, said the mother rabbit
in complete control of the rabbit universe

while I sing to keep you
as barely awake as possible

From your sideways gaze through the rails
my body shaped like wicker
& glowing in the corner
ghosts over to the last thing
you shall hear

if I have to sing until midnight
said the mother rabbit
you shall hear my pure self

POSSIBLE

If all of the parents
love their children
the way we love you
then the world is far more
unbearable than
we think
in our newly shuddering skins
raw as adults
trusting in you to change us

A WOMAN GOES FOR A WALK

A WOMAN GOES FOR A WALK

Hers

A heterosexual couple and their single lesbian friend walk with the couple's baby in a stroller to an art gallery opening, where the lesbian is asked several times if the baby is hers.

Food

A woman goes on a walk with her baby in a stroller, to deliver a manuscript to the arts council. On her way she gets some food at a deli and goes to a park bench to eat it. Two men are having a conversation at a nearby picnic table. One of them wants to leave his wife. The woman listens so intently that when she gets up to go she forgets her manuscript on the bench. She thinks about her husband and wonders whether he would leave her. The baby is sleeping.

Loaf

A woman goes for a walk with her baby in a stroller and decides to take a shortcut through an alleyway. In the alley a man and woman are semi-sleeping, drunk. They have a mirror and a loaf of Wonderbread. The woman watches them so blankly she doesn't notice when the baby's rattle falls onto the ground. She proceeds to a parking lot that is usually a thoroughfare to her street but today is locked. When she turns around and heads back for the street she sees that one of the drunks is clasping the rattle.

Hurt

A woman goes for a walk with her baby in a stroller and when she gets home she finds her gay friend has left a box of flowers he has grown for her on her porch. The woman procrastinates planting the seedlings and a couple of weeks later they die. The woman is too embarrassed to tell her friend, so she tells him they are flourishing. Meanwhile, he has learned that he is HIV-positive but he is not ready to tell the woman, since he fears she will become distant. He keeps saying he wants to visit her garden to see how the flowers are doing, and the woman keeps making up excuses. Finally, he drops by one day and discovers her garden in full bloom. He makes the assumption that a particularly bright patch is the group of flowers he gave her. She blurts out that the tray he brought died. He is visibly hurt and blurts out he is very ill. She becomes very incensed that he would not have told her such an important thing earlier. Just then her husband comes home and rushes out into the back garden laughing at a joke he heard on his car radio.

City

On a walk with her baby in the stroller, a young woman remembers driving with her male friend from their hometown to a much larger city. En route, on an isolated stretch of highway, another car begins to tailgate them, honking. The woman becomes frightened. She tells her friend to keep driving at all costs. The car moves alongside them and tries to butt them onto the shoulder. They both start to panic. Driving the car is a woman in a jean jacket. A baby is slumped in a car seat beside her. The woman motions for them to pull over, gesturing with one hand wildly at the child. When they finally stop to find out what the matter is the woman says the baby is sick and requires medical attention but that she is an illegal immigrant and cannot take the baby to the hospital. She begs them to take the baby in for her. The woman and her friend decide to risk it. The woman trails them in her car to a clinic in the next town. When they finally come out of the examination room, the woman is nowhere to be found.

Porn

A woman goes for a walk with a very young baby in a stroller and suddenly feels a light rain begin. She jangles into a hardware store where two men seated at the counter look up startled from a porn magazine they are reading together. The woman masks her shock, and the men in return attempt to continue looking coolly at the magazine. The baby awakens and begins to cry. The woman, flustered by the baby's distress, sits down on a paint-spattered stool and automatically opens her shirt to nurse. After a few minutes she regains her composure and asks the men if there is a telephone she can use. Engrossed again in the magazine, the two men do not hear her. Just then the baby bites the woman's nipple and she shrieks. The men look up to the sight of drops of blood on her exposed breast. She asks if either of them has a Band-aid.

Luck

One Friday morning, a woman goes for a walk with her baby in a stroller to pay household bills at a nearby bank machine. The machine quite unexpectedly swallows her card and she lines up for help from a customer service agent. There are numerous people queued up at the counter occupying all of the tellers. No one comes to serve her. She gets very impatient and begins to fume. Suddenly an elderly woman patron in the lineup falls down and a crowd gathers around her. Fire trucks arrive and some paramedics rush into the bank. Despite the crisis, the woman continues to sulk about the lack of service and curses under her breath. She laments how she never gets time to herself, and that this simple task has eaten up her whole morning. Further she doesn't know how she can possibly get by without her bank card. She leaves the bank not caring about the elderly woman's state. When she gets home, she calls her father who lives in the suburbs to borrow some money. The father is quite sarcastic about how the woman cannot manage her money, that overspending must be the reason her card was confiscated.

She tries to explain that it was fully the machine's error and bad luck, plain and simple, that these things just happen to her.

True

A woman finds herself to be overly self-critical and her husband to be overly self-congratulatory. She muses while she takes her baby for a walk in the stroller that perhaps the two of them have been drawn together to learn from each other's qualities. She hopes that even if this is not true, their child will internalize both self-criticality and self-congratulation, and in this way become balanced, happy and responsible.

Hold

A white woman goes for a lengthy walk with her baby in a stroller and begins to notice she is hungry. Once the baby has fallen to sleep, she covers the carriage with a light blanket and goes into a small Japanese café. Two women are hand-rolling and cutting sushi. Suddenly the woman realizes she has left her wallet at another shop a block away. She impulsively asks the two women to watch the baby while she runs to retrieve her lost wallet. When she returns, five complete strangers are gathered about the baby singing a lullaby in unison and chuckling quietly. Neither of the two women she recognizes is there. When she interrupts, the group stares at her without speaking, and two men maintain their hold on the stroller handle. As a last resort the woman pulls a photograph of the baby from her wallet and displays it broadly. The group begins laughing and touching her arm, saying the child is exceptionally beautiful and that she must be very proud.

Plot

A woman goes for a walk with her baby asleep in a stroller and ends up at a public beach. She sits close to the water trying to read a mystery and after a few moments drops the book into the sand. She is so tired from walking the baby that she picks the book up and resumes reading without brushing off the grains of sand. She continues reading several chapters right through the tiny granules, and feels pleased to be following the plot so well. That evening after supper, her boyfriend asks her how her reading is going, and the woman stutters that she can't remember anything but a sandbar and the smell of hotdogs, although she is sure the novel is set in Venice.

THE DIFFERENCE BETWEEN DAWN AND DUSK

ARMS

(1989)

Perhaps the blossoms crested
past the safe buoy of your elbow one night
on a tenth birthday — I admit
I may have been absent or dreaming
as I am prone — and you bypassed a mirror
caught the rose bruise encroaching
   your body a peninsula of blood.
Perhaps your whole life became red for a moment.

From the backseat, their adult necks were inscrutable
and our eyes
saw this together, absorbed
sisterhood. Odd how their ignorance
stirred us. What it stirred.
My scrawny arm held to yours at the wrist
our pyjama sleeves scrunched back like tourniquets
and your lips, your tongue, executing their
lamprey task (assured, enviable suction)
teaching me even this;
                        and then switching —
my smaller mouth on you, for you,
testing the purple points upward
your skin's surface tasting russet, like broth
a burst-heart tattoo
our best yet.

Other times I'm struck remembering
your clear ear for flood warnings, the marsupial
quiet of your thumb-sucking habit
while I fantasized like mad, soundless

our night room like a movie screen
suffocating under kisses.
I'm unsurprised by our sameness.
The need for insides of things, and excellent radar.

But now, your permission is unasked. Your body
is something lonely in my mouth like words
speaking a proxy heat. To let go
of even the arm you put away, white,
tight-buttoned against sunburn and comparisons.
Being ten to my eight must have unnerved you.
Your whole life in the car mirror
suspended between their stark, unspeaking necks
and my blue-veined
enthusiasm.

EPIDURAL

When you put your hand in the cool river
it soon touches bottom, blindly fumbling for something solid
like you, after the two minutes of our twins'
coming, probing the sandpile of my crumpled abdominal wall
as if to urge my spinal column out of the soft terrain
shake the sinew loose in brash daylight
see, here is her nerve canal
here is the sum of her future
probable gross motor interests
how she'll want to get up from that table
and walk again, naturally

With your fingers that deep
you prop her upright as if, I'm not sure,
erecting a slippery deciduous sapling
on your property, where you've always
imagined one, in the frame of the kitchen's rear window
a shaded hush unlike the anesthetist's
blunt bargain:
if you move now it is extremely dangerous
if you fail to hold this arch I cannot promise
anything good . . .

Cleaving to the hand you've agreed
to let me suck under into my panic
my arbour of trust in you, then, for that
inconceivably still moment, she will hold tight
to the anchor of your knuckles
will despair there that she could
ever move an inch, a breath,
a hair's motion, or perish

Sometimes I have liked penetration
from behind, even games of anonymity
and surrender, but with the needle poised to enter
the exact space between vertebrae, between
the two pieces of the phrase "extremely
dangerous," glare of harsh
operative lighting, she would prefer
a safe word, a garden
an absence of choices
just water, sand bottom, open palms
a legacy of slow walks together along nighttime
sidestreets, canopied by horse chestnuts and silver maples
your fingertips playing up and down her back
like on the neck of an evening cello
taking care to miss the still-sore pricked spot
where the freezing poured in, mint spear, chilled
gin, insurgent sap rippling through the nerve tree
that feeds her — she hasn't been that cold
    on the inside before —
the way gazpacho runs down your throat
the way feeling resumes in a frost-bitten hand
never to take it for granted
never to count on the easy return
from deadened to alive again

Justifiable fear and hope, the double-breasted
hallmarks of how some women agree
to push the rest of the world forth, plainly,
with pain and leaning over into cold rivers
touching bottom and folding the body back
into ordinary ritual —
fumbling again to sit, stretch, shit,
wipe up after bleeding, make milk,
coat the nipples with lanolin, squeeze shut
the adult teeth for those first few sharp-gummed suckles
how tender she is, has been,

I am more tender, even, since the epidural
and now, standing tall to glimpse
the lush bush of white peonies
just blossomed, all at once, sentient, awake
my second day home

TWINNING

for *Clea and Silas*

1.
When the abdomen becomes an access route
we know nature rates second.
Necessity decides more than is easily
accepted. When the twins are lifted
out from the shrinking womb onto the stainless table
they meet the world that names them: to warm up
their bellies are swaddled, small lips suck oxygen,
they and she are linked like mammals, good colostrum.
The i.v. coagulates bleeding, to do this
effectively the valves must shut, then open,
must press upon the mother.

2.
She half-sleeps, moulded to her twins
each elbow propping one midriff, scrunched up
lower bodies tucked under hospital linens, digesting how
familial landscapes are pervious and subject to
overflow.

Earlier she stumbled out to the antiseptic cubicle
linoleum cold, darkness stirrupy
through which bittersweet cries cut
her abdomen quivering, in shock,
new stitches sensible as a morse code
banishing sense from the pelvic floor.

She thinks of a double suckle
any position that can hold both babies
at the larger tips of her body and shake, in fact, shake up
her letdown.

3.
When laughter dodges through their inner eyes
it is as if the gods dance
madly ecstatic. And when you lift the chests
you feel the hearts' weight, substantial
yet big enough only to pump
thimblefuls of blood around.
Physics cannot cure such a riddle.
Not books, nor brains, nor cash
siphoned from the universe by someone
else's smarts. Just the slow soak
of foamy, carbon-married love. She can't
bear telling this, though, and whites out
the voice purpling it.

The poet prides herself
on such deflations.

4.
She angles the mirror low to check her incision line,
assess how much skin the sutures take.
She represses the truth, finding the bandage
bulging up to one eye, hiding like a doctor
the irrefutable damage — there it is, over
four inches wide! And there! The *mess* of her!

Months pass like this . . .

5.
When their abdomens hush
she becomes fully confessional.

6.
When imperfect tricks to charm
sleep incline her toward the mind's
death she goes nuts. Exhaustion is like this
shadow of the civil, near indeed.

To tuck the nipples into their mouths
and nurse them together, this is what the twin books
bitch is easy, nine times a day
despite a lack of rest so militaristic
thought sifts through her like sugar, white drift
of all cells, the milk spurting.

7.
When she holds their small foreheads
they have the curve of family to offer
fervent composite of her own and his foreheads
and the first son's, whom they are thinking of, always

8.
       thos(e)
twin-bor(n)
       no(t)
     quit(e)
   simila(r)

9.
Shit and soothers, hurrying
to best endure the tenacity
of her offspring, nightly snubbed
stomach unloved because healed in
under duress, what consciousness
can survive unaided by
solitude, sometimes, she craves herself
more than —

10.

       he
       she
       he
       he
       she

From that moment
they all swim toward each other, five whorled
tips of a star-shaped anchor
cast out, the water ringing and fluttery,
like a fine dream of hoops
through which they are bound
for the centre of the world

BISEXUAL PROVISO FOR A NEW LOVER

As it is a matter of every neck torquing
toward or away from drifts of motion
we live in, unparalyzable storyboard
of any skin's surface,
each hair aware of flux and following it as
a dream's descent is ushered, exactly who
plays the part of the lover is moot.
Can't you agree to this, then, if your
body fits me, I will luckily wear it
on the inside, a shirt turned
the wrong way round, seams to the outside
and evidentiary: how we make
who we should become unnaturally
stitched. So I open you up
undress you fully down to the naked
state of sexed muscle, swollen & kaleidoscoping
through the hackneyed carpentry of gender we're
used to, fitting bolts to nuts, screws and pins
knowing his or her bodies are not
the thing so much as a general
inclination toward the laying of palms,
greedy, into whatever pocket of magnets
you are secreting, alongside the hip bone,
carved shelf of tissue that leads to the pubis,
that proceeds inside to heat, moisture, metallic smells
of coupling, I must be dreaming again of
who you will be when I meet you
in the close quarters, wee hours, the fickle moments
of my impending arousal. & it is imperative
that the ridges of unique fingertips
leave their wet trace on my torso
that they touch down like rainfall
and the cool breeze that sweeps it — this whisper
of presence — away or toward wanting
you back again.

FICKLE MOMENTS

i.

again. rainfall that of moments
smells that greedy, palms, pins
used undress up outside the
can't moot surface, of as
lover bisexual

ii.

again. that moments that palms,
used up the moot. of
lover bisexual as surface, can't
outside undress pins greedy, smells
of rainfall

iii.

again. wanting whisper rainfall torso
fingertips imperative moments you of
smells pubis, bone, magnets palms,
general not pins we're kaleidoscoping
naked up unnaturally make outside
turned it your moot. who
as surface, storyboard motion torquing
lover

again. torso fingertips of smells
palms, general kaleidoscoping naked outside
turned who as torquing lover

iv.

again. of moments greedy, palms,
undress up can't moot. as
lover bisexual of surface, the
outside used pins that smells
that rainfall

again. undress lover outside that
palms, as the smells rainfall

V.

as motion we surface, each
who plays your body turned
the make who up undress
kaleidoscoping through pins knowing general
inclination magnets you pubis, that
of who moments of fingertips
leave rainfall and wanting you
again.